# Jim Edgar

Hodder & Stoughton
LONDON SYDNEY AUCKLAND

British Library Cataloguing in Publication Data
A record for this book is available from the British Library

ISBN 0 340 86373 0

Printed and bound in Great Britain by CPI Bath

The paper used in this book is a natural recyclable product made from wood grown in sustainable forests. The hard coverboard is recycled.

Hodder & Stoughton
A Division of Hodder Headline Ltd
338 Euston Road
London NW1 3BH

www.madaboutbooks.com

# A word...

**I**f history has taught us anything it is that cat views us as creatures ignoble, if not expendable. cat has been stuck with Homo Sapiens Sapiens since recorded history. Yes, there are two 'Sapiens' in our name. If you did not know this, cat probably hates you for it.

As any cat owner can tell you, the smugness on their whiskered faces can only mean disdain for you and your kind. Behind the dry, patronizing smirk is a mastermind of terror gazing at you with pity in its eyes. why would you deserve anything more than pity for the bald monkey you are?

'But wait, Jim', you stammer. 'My cat loves me. can you not see it smiling when I bring it fresh food and cream?' Yes, I know cat cuddles and purrs. If someone bought me food and drink each day while I sat in my pile of shredded fur, I would smile too, sucker.

Though it appears cute and cuddly and makes us 'aaah' as a kitten, treachery lies buried within. Memories of past injustices awaken latent evil. cat becomes sloth-like, introverted, self-centred and finally vengeful.

And why shouldn't it? what if it was you who was dressed in a red and green-striped stocking with a little elf hat every christmas, chasing a laser pointer around the room for the amusement of others. or you, waiting for a half-drunken ape to open your Xmas 'gift' of tender meat treats...and being held aloft and treated like a newborn child. And your name is Poop Noodle to boot.

3

But cat plays along, following your script, while it plans and schemes. And in the end, you lose, you always lose.

cat is harder on the wallet than an ex-spouse could ever be. If cat were a country it would probably boast the largest economy on the planet. And all the while laughing silently as it dupes you into trading your earnings for food, milk, catnip, a warm fleecy bed and that stupid christmas hat.

I am not talking only about hard cash but also the currency of the soul, love. Like a psychic sponge, cat absorbs your soul and offers in return less emotion than a poster of The Terminator.

All cat-afflicted souls have my utmost compassion. As a tribute to them, I offer this collection of pictures from their lives. They are a work in progress, compiled from the hard-working stiffs who would consider themselves 'owned' by their ward. Visitors to my Internet website, **www.mycathatesyou.com**, have taken me into confidence at the risk of life and limb to help spread the word. I salute them for their bravery in combat.

This compendium is the result of meticulously filtering thousands of photographs according to only one criterion, truth. It is a sad and simple truth:

# Your cat hates you.

Enjoy.

Jim

# Agnes

Agnes hates **YOU** and **EVERYBODY**.

# Menace

I poop, I kill, I stalk, all in my little hat.

# corrie

corrie enjoys peeing in your pint.

# Graciandlola

Think of us as good cop...bad cop.
But there ain't no good cop.

# Aly

Prostrate before me or I will be forced to use your face as a scratching post!

# Angror

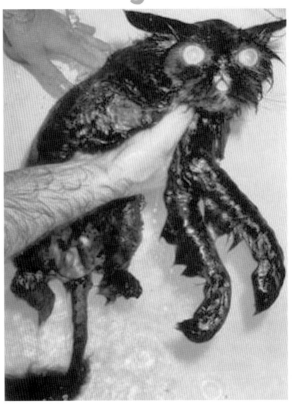

Revenge is a dish best served in the bath.

# Gertie

Gertie 'Muscles' Vintano reminds you
your payment is late.

# coffee kittens

We are almost done making your 'coffee'.

# Ransom (Nova is the white one)

What's your problem? It's only illegal in the South.

# cutie Pops

Mr cutie Pops will undoubtedly become
intolerant of the giggling fools that surround
him. He will deal with them, indeed.

# Luukie

Tired of playing 'Knights of the
Round Table' with you, Luukie starts
looking for a lance.

# Q-Ball

Dry food my ass...come here he
who can't see in the dark.

# Psycho

Once I get focus, there will be
**MUCH** hell to pay.

# Poppy

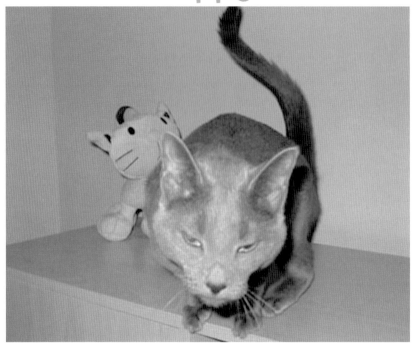

Poppy is a paranoid amphetamine junkie because her owners wisely hid her catnip.

# Friseminine

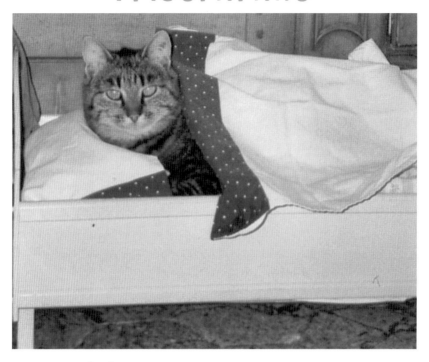

I don't know anything about any child.
Please get me a lawyer.

# Georgia

Her mother had always warned her that rolling her eyes in annoyance would get her stuck one day.

# Blarney

Blarney rivals Saddam in crimes
against humanity.

# Couch Potato

Having killed his owners, Couch Potato
settles down to watch some TV.

# Harry

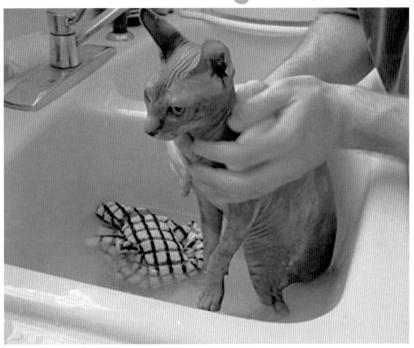

Unsure of his ultimate fate,
Harry takes a bath like a good cat until
he can turn the tables.

# Gozde

oh, look at me! I'm a human, wheee!

# Diggler

Even in his sleep he attacks without warning.

# Manson

I am trying to find your self-esteem.
You should thank me.

This is for taking me to 'cowboy night' at your gay disco.

# Pharoah

What's so funny? Who's Marty Feldman?

# Abelard

Inwardly seething with fury
because his Jedi Mind Trick has not
turned him into a cougar yet.

# Bailey

Put me down, newbie, I can't get to my tequila shots.

# Elvis

Target acquired, claws loaded, it's **GO** time.

# Herbert

For the last time, where is the kitty porn?

# Nermal

Do you see? I have to wear this
tinfoil hat to prevent your black hole of
intelligence from stealing my I.Q.

# Pajama

I hate you and all clipper-wielding,
beauty school drop-outs like you.

# Tiger

Yes, you are up shit creek.

No, you have no paddle.

# Sleeman

Named after the beer he loves to drink,
we keep him drunk so he doesn't
kill us in our sleep.

# Snide

My turban is at the cleaners, okay? Infidel.

# Rusty

Goddamit, whersh my **VODKA** ! you
punk assh gimme my vodka back, I will **KILL**
you in shirty sheconds!

# Snuggles

He hates the bullshit name you gave him.

# Badass

where the fuck are my bits?!

# Hexx

is this supposed to be a joke or something?

# Harry²

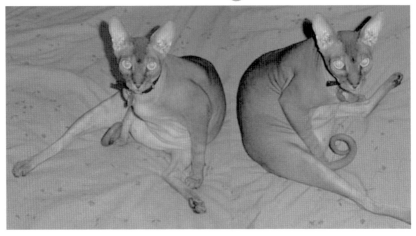

This is Harry and Evil Harry from the Evil Dimension. Which one hates you more?

# Weetabix

Don't let the wise-old-cat beard fool you.

He hates without remorse or emotion.

A true demon from the East.

# Zack

Twisted Zack takes his hate for you to a
whole new angle.

# Siva

She wants everyone to see her
intense hatred for anything
that deals with christmas.

# Rusty Noodle

The Russian spy does not love you, comrade.

# Galen and Shelby

We are sweet and innocent, come here! We are sweet and innocent, come here!

# Dink

Only one man has ever tried to pet Dink, a generous, one-armed man who used to order rounds of beers for his three friends by raising four fingers. Now he orders two at a time.

# Einstein

This is one wet pussy I would **NOT** let into the bedroom.

# Barney

This does not sate my hunger for flesh.
It is not even my birthday.

# Blaze

You do not want to be the one to let
**THIS** cat out of the bag.

# camden

Feh! When they find your body, they will deem it 'suicide by being an asshole'.

# candace

Count to three...slowly.
Yes...yes...sleepy...sleepy.

# Godzilla

Even a master of evil has to have a sidekick.

# Akira

Akira deals with **you** from on high.

# Black Bugger

Feeling bored?  Stuck in a rut?
Try demonic possession.  It worked for me!

# Anastasia

Who's Bob Hope? Why is everyone laughing at me?

# Angst

Yes, I know you're gay. You don't have to shove it in my face.

# Ashes

I said I was to look like caesar,
not Thora Hird.

# Balt

Ah, this time of year again. I wish I had
a pitchfork to shove up your arse.

# Baxter

Yo, yo, yo! Respect this shit, motherfucker.

# chairman Maow

Drinking Teacher's...it doesn't get
much worse than that.

# Beardogg

You know, they shot my son, Sonny,
thirty times. Me, I'm still walking.

# crazyboy

This bastardo scares even al-Qaeda.

# Evil Olive

This is Olive, the evil Sphinx kitten.
She hates cutesy puppies.

# Fatty Sherwin

Peel me a prawn, pathetic bald slave.

# Max

No, I don't have any booze.
And stop calling me Churchill.

# Frederic

On a good day Frederic will scream, hiss and claw at you. On a bad day he will rip open your flesh and yowl with delight at your suffering.

# Frog

And you thought the madness would stop
when you fed it.

# Gizmo

Hatred, in its purest, oil-like and foul-smelling form, oozes from every single pore...

# Hallow Elvis

Elvis wants you to know that he hates
you because you like Halloween,
you trick-or-treatin' jerks!

# Iza

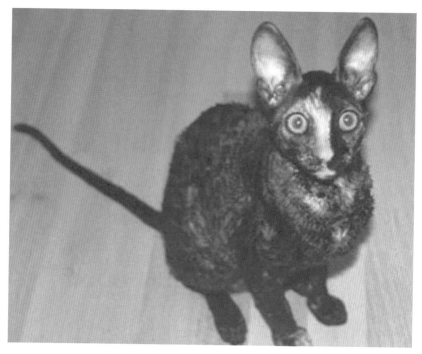

what the **HELL** is recombinant DNA?
what the **HELL** is a fruit bat?

# Alfi

Alfi **IS** the weapons of mass destruction.

# Jack

Jack makes wood-rope in the old style,
out of splayed wood. Later he wants
to make bone-rope. (Get it?)

# Nerhmal-Now

I wanted a trampoline for christmas.
Now I have to bounce your body parts
off something else.

# OScar

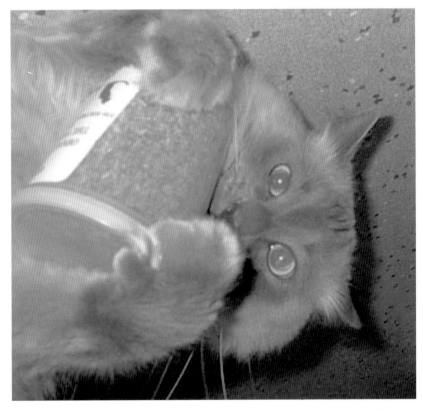

arrr! open this fucking thing, will you?

# Piersilvio

Put me down or I will hide your Viagra and
Britney Spears videos.

# Jeanlucpicard

In this prison **EVERYTHING** has its price.

# Kashmere

so **THIS** is why you are an asshole...

# Lexi

Lexi regrets living in a house full of doctors.

# Livia

I was supposed to transport into a drawer
of lingerie, not your ass shorts.

# Lola

You go to Japan, and all I get is
**THIS** fucking thing?

# Marco

I don't care what time it is. Give me victuals
or join the castrati choir.

# Marcus

Digging on the Good Life,
Marcus awaits his salmon.

# Memphis

He does not appreciate your
tribute to firefighters.

# Miss Kitty

**NONE SHALL PASS!**

# Mojo

This cat hates angles.

# Morgan

I drink to make **YOU** interesting.

# Mr Fabulous

Mr Fabulous is his name and he hates you
so much that it's making him go
cross-eyed with rage.

# Harley

She's looking for small
mammals - hide your baby.

# Noelle

I found it in a Paris tunnel - so what?

# Patrick

I hate you for bombing my town in Croatia.

# Sake

Even Spiderman is not safe against this
terror from the East.

# Sans

She hates you and your music taste too.

# satchmo

He hates you for feeding him
'weight control' food.

# Satan's Little Helpers

We can't do much to you yet but these claws
are getting bigger and stronger every day!

# Zoey

Zoey hates you for being jealous
of her beauty.

# Shelby

By now you should know the
routine - be hated!

# The Shower Kitty

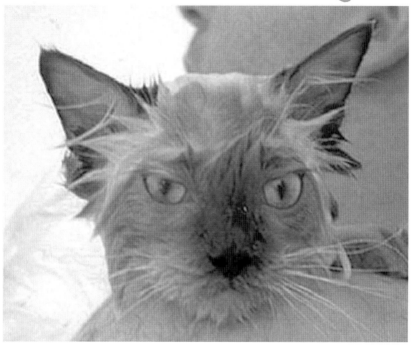

My haiku: I sit on shoulder. You laugh and mock my wetness. Your bits for dinner.

# Simone

Go ahead. Turn on the water, jerkoff.
I've already peed on your toothbrush.
It was totally worth it.

# sitka

He hates you for coming to the book-of-the-month club without having read the freaking **BOOK!**

# Suzi Wong

Suzi does **NOT** like you laughing when she tries to wash her seven bellies.

# Tessa

The oldest trick in the book.

# The cats

This menagerie of evil speaks for itself.
Be fooled **NOT**. Do whatever they say.

# Tweeg

Tweeg hates you for calling her
'Sammy Davis' and 'Columbo'.

# Vax

Thug life.

# Weezy

The penultimate master of evil, only Lucifer
can bring you more sorrow.

# Yoshimi

Yoshimi hates you so much he scared
the pants off you!

# Zachy

zachy hates you for staring at his sexy neuter scars.

# Zix

The news is bad I'm afraid...looks like
you don't have long to live.

# Yuri

Like a grenade, if you let go...say
goodbye to hand.

# Leroy

Leroy is just fed up with your crap.